希望之光

the Light of Hope

The Light of Hope: Pearls of Wisdom by the Venerable Master Hua
Illustrations and Reflections by Cathie Chen.
希望之光

Published and translated by:
Buddhist Text Translation Society
1777 Murchison Drive
Burlingame, CA 94010-4504
www.drba.org

© 2006 Buddhist Text Translation Society
Dharma Realm Buddhist University
Dharma Realm Buddhist Association

11 10 09 08 07 06 10 9 8 7 6 5 4 3 2 1

ISBN 986-7328-25-6
Printed in Taiwan

一個年青的畫家，

從來沒有見過宣公上人，

以後也不可能見到上人，

卻在上人的法雨中找到智慧之源；

上人的教法，沒有國界、沒有男女老少，超越時空。

相信上人的法語配以凱西的作品，

將廣泛地為年青一代燃起希望之光。

Although this young artist has never met the Venerable Master Hua,

and will never meet him in the future,

she has found a source of wisdom in the Venerable Master's Dharma Rain.

In the Venerable Master's teachings,

there is no differentiation among nations,

between men and women, and between the elderly and the young.

Rather, his teachings transcend time and space.

We believe that a work of the Venerable Master's Dharma

talks accompanied by Cathie's art will ignite

a far-reaching light of hope for the young generation.

宣化上人
是我的師公。
我尊稱他
"宣公上人"

凱西・陳

Master Hua is my teacher's teacher.
I respectfully refer to him
as the "Venerable Master Hua."

Cathie Chen

福不可以享盡，

享盡就沒有福了。

苦可以受盡，
受盡就沒有苦了。

我想，
苦差事一次做完
就輕鬆了。

你真傻，
為什麼不先
去玩呢？

: I think an unpleasant chore should be finished first, in one go; then I can relax.

: You are really silly! Why don't you go out and play first?

亂西想

The Venerable Master Hua said:

Don't become attached to your blessings,
because once they're exhausted,
you'll have none.
Take all the suffering that comes to you,
because once you've endured it all,
you'll suffer no more.

03

Mom: You haven't finished cleaning, so you can't rest yet!

🟡 : Oh, no!

🔴 : I am done!

Cathie's Reflections

有憂愁才有恐懼，
沒有憂愁就沒有什麼恐懼。

沒有自私心也就沒有恐懼心，

不爭、不貪．不求．不自私．不自利．不打妄語，

這樣就不需要怕了。

我呀！
什麼都不害怕。
因為，
沒有什麼是我非得到不可的。

 : I am not afraid of anything, because there is nothing that I can't do without.

凱西想

The Venerable Master Hua said:

Worry gives rise to fear.
If you have no worries,
you won't fear anything.
If you are unselfish,
then you have nothing to fear.
Indeed, there is nothing to be afraid of
if you avoid contending, are not greedy,
do not seek, are not selfish,
do not pursue personal advantages,
and do not lie.

沒有事憂愁；所以沒有恐懼；
所以身心平靜。

● : When there are no worries,
   there is no fear, and then the body and mind are peaceful.

Cathie's Reflections

宣公上人說

古人說：「居鄰必擇，交友必慎。」
交朋友一定要選擇良友，
處處互助，不可狼狽為奸。
若交無益之友，令你往下流走，
甚至身敗名裂，永不翻身，而到地獄去。

不聽你的。
我是要好好
　　看書的。

走嘛，
來玩啊！
又沒人管著你。

● : Let's go and play! There's no one watching us.

● : I am not listening to you. I am going to behave and read my book.

凱西想

The Venerable Master Hua said:

The ancients said,
"Choose your neighbors and friends with care."
Pick friends who are good and can help
each other out in every way.
Don't get involved with people who
are cruel and heartless.
Friends who are bad influences
can drag you down to the point
that you lose your fortune
and reputation forever and end up in the hells.

11

● : I think what needs to be done should be finished diligently, at one go.

● : I'm not that dumb. It's more important to play first!

Cathie's Reflections

宣公上人說

佛法就是心法，
你心裡沒有私心、妄想、狂心、野性，
這就是佛法；
你若有習氣、心病、狂心、野性、妄想，
這就叫「魔法」。

「佛」就是屬於善念的、清淨的；
「魔」就是屬於惡念的、污染的、不清淨的。

你啊！
別老想覇著
那麼多。

: Don't try to grab everything for yourself!

The Venerable Master Hua said:

The Buddhadharma is the Dharma of the mind.
If your mind has no selfish thoughts,
idle thoughts, deranged thoughts,
and uncivilized instincts,
then your mind is the Buddhadharma.
However, if you have bad habits, faults,
deranged thoughts, uncivilized instincts,
and idle thoughts, then this is called "demon-dharma."
A Buddha has kind and pure thoughts,
while a demon has evil, defiled and impure thoughts.

拖著那麼多
那麼重，
難怪你哪也去不成，
什麼都做不了。

累～

: It's really tiring to be dragging along all these heavy things!
  No wonder you can't go anywhere or do anything.

Cathie's Reflections

譬如菩提是水，煩惱是冰；
水就是冰，冰就是水，
水冰同骨豐，沒有兩樣。
寒時，水結成冰；
熱時，冰化為水。

比方說：
手心代表
　　煩惱。

⬤ ： For example, the palm of my hand represents affliction …

凱西想

The Venerable Master Hua said:

If enlightenment is likened to water,
then affliction can be likened to ice.
Water is ice, and ice is water,
for they are of the same substance.
When it is cold, water freezes into ice,
and when it is hot, ice melts into water.

舒羽轉過來，
手背是智慧。

● : ... turn it over, and the back of my hand is wisdom.

Cathie's Reflections

宣公上人說

換言之，有煩惱時，水結成冰；
無煩惱時，冰化為水。
這個道理很容易明白。

但要說起來，
還不都是
這双手？

⬤ : However, isn't it still the same pair of hands?

凱西想

The Venerable Master Hua said:

In other words,
when we get afflicted,
water freezes into ice.
In contrast,
when we have no afflictions,
ice turns into water.
This principle is easy to understand.

所以啊我們！
要轉煩惱為菩提。

 : Therefore, we should turn affliction into Bodhi!

Cathie's Reflections

宣公上人說

事來則應，事過則靜。

25

鏡子。
Mirror

我在鏡子前，
鏡中有我。

: When I stand in front of the mirror, there is my reflection in the mirror.

凱西想

The Venerable Master Hua said:

When a matter arises,
respond to it appropriately;

When the matter passes,
return to stillness.

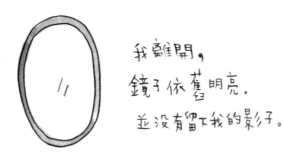

我離開，
鏡子依舊明亮．
並沒有留下我的影子。

● : When I leave, the mirror returns to its brightness;
it no longer contains my reflection.

Cathie's Reflections

活一天要有一天的意義，
不要被妄想壓倒，
終日在妄想中打轉，
這豈不是愚人嗎？
想些不可能的事，
想些不必要的事，
這簡直是和自己過不去，
自討苦吃。

怎麼啦?
又不開心?

我不會飛。

● : What's wrong? Why are you unhappy?

● : I can't fly.

飲西想

The Venerable Master Hua said:

We should live each day
in a meaningful way.
Don't let idle thoughts overwhelm you.
To be influenced by idle thoughts
all day long is simply to be a fool.
Thinking about impossible
and unnecessary things,
one merely creates problems for oneself
and asks for trouble.

● : Why do you always wish for impossible things and create problems for yourself?

● : I can't help it! I think this way!

Cathie's Reflections

人持戒，
就是清淨自在，
將自性黑暗一掃而空。
人若不守戒，
烏雲就重重無盡，
一日不守戒，
一日就多生出烏雲。

打個比方。

每天才擦擦鏡子，
鏡子就明亮。

● ：Let's take an example.
　　If we wipe clean the mirror every day, then the mirror will remain bright.

勸西想

The Venerable Master Hua said:

A person who observes the moral
precepts is pure and at ease,
able to sweep away the darkness
covering up his original nature.
If one fails to observe the precepts,
then dark clouds gather endlessly.
For every day one fails to observe the precepts,
a day's worth of dark clouds will accumulate.

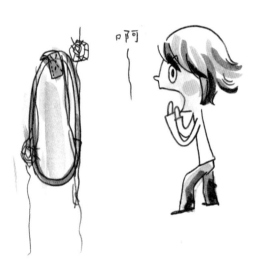

啊———

那麼，
像這樣，
很久都不曾擦拭，
鏡子就...

: Ah, but if we don't clean the mirror for a long time, it will look like this . . .

Cathie's Reflections

宣公上人說

從自己修身起，
在內心與自己不爭，
則一切發狂妄想皆不起，
平平靜靜，這就是真的快樂。
你自己平靜快樂，
就能影響旁人都平靜快樂。

哼！

你老是亂發脾氣。
旁人全都受你波及。

- ： You always lose your temper for no reason and affect the people around you.
- ： Grumble.

凱西想

The Venerable Master Hua said:

As a result of your cultivation,
you will be at peace with yourself
and no deranged or idle thoughts will arise.
This peace and serenity is true happiness.
When you are peaceful and happy,
you can influence the people around you
to become peaceful and happy, too.

但若你開心了，
鳥兒齊歌唱，
花也特別香。

🔴 : But when you are happy,
the birds sing together and the flowers smell especially nice.

Cathie's Reflections

自滿的人一定不會有什麼成就，
人要「有若無、實若虛」。

● : Do you want to study with me?

● : I don't have the time!

The Venerable Master Hua said:

A person who is content has no ambitions.
One should
"possess something as if it were nothing,
and regard one's attainments as empty."

不瞞你說，
我這個人呵呵！
什麼都懂呢！

這樣啊...
那麼你就什麼
都學不到了！

⬤ : To tell you the truth, I already know everything!

⬤ : Oh . . . then you won't be able to learn anything!

Cathie's Reflections

你有信心，

就能打破一切困難的境界。

一切唯心造，

你心裡覺得它困難就困難，

覺得容易就容易。

我知道。
我可以突破重圍。

: I know I can break through this barrier.

凱西想

The Venerable Master Hua said:

You only need to have faith,
and then you can break through
all difficult states.
"Everything is made from the mind alone."
If you think something is difficult,
then it will be difficult;
if you think it is easy, it will be easy.

我深信
我可以！

● : I truly believe that I can!

Cathie's Reflections

宣公上人說

你心裏有鬼，就是人怕鬼；
你心裏沒鬼，就是鬼怕人。

: I am so scared!

: If you don't let your imagination run wild,
  you won't be scared any more.

The Venerable Master Hua said:

If there is a ghost in your mind,
you will be afraid of ghosts;
but, if there is no ghost in your mind,
then ghosts will be afraid of you.

好的，壞的，
全都是我想出来的。

: Both good and bad are products of my thoughts.

Cathie's Reflections

沒有自私心，
便什麼事情都不會和他人計較，
或亂發脾氣。

: I should put down the mirror in my hand,
and not care so much about the "I" in the mirror.

The Venerable Master Hua said:

An unselfish person would never,
under any circumstance,
argue with others nor wildly
lose his temper.

🔴 : You can eat the big one!

🟡 : Wow!

Cathie's Reflections

宣公上人說

我們信佛的人，不應該迷信。
什麼是迷信？
就是迷糊裏迷糊塗的亂信，
別人說什麼就信，信迷了。

「迷信」還不打緊，
最怕是「信迷」，
信那迷亂顛倒的外道。

閱讀經典，
是非常重要的事。

: It is very important to read the Sutras (Buddhist scriptures).

The Venerable Master Hua said:

People who believe in the Buddha
should not be superstitious.
Being superstitious means being reckless
and confused in your belief.
You simply believe in whatever people say,
and you end up all muddled.
However, being superstitious is still not
that serious. It is a lot worse if you believe
in the deluded teachings of heterodox cults.

經書上沒說的，
上人沒說的，
就絕不去亂信一通。

 : If something is not stated by the Sutras or the Venerable Master,
then we definitely should not be confused into believing such a statement.

Cathie's Reflections

宣公上人說

所謂「緊了繃，慢了鬆，不緊不慢才成功。」
天天這樣的用功，
時時這樣的用功，
也不緊，也不慢，
久而久之，
功夫就相應。

走了那麼地遠，
你怎麼能
不喘也不累？

我啊，
一路上
都用不快也不慢
的速度走著。

: How come you're not out of breath or tired after walking so far?

: It's because I maintain a walking speed that is neither too fast nor too slow.

凱西想

The Venerable Master Hua said:

It is said of stringed instruments,
"If the string is too tight,
it will break. If it is too loose,
it will produce a dull sound.
The instrument will work only if the string
is neither too tight nor too loose.
" If you cultivate according to this advice
every day and every moment,
being neither too tense nor too lax,
then in the course of time you
will accomplish something.

不心急，
也不怠惰，
才能走得長。

● : We can walk far only by being neither in a hurry nor idle.

Cathie's Reflections

宣公上人說

若心的開關不打開，
就是有佛光也照不到。

65

不打開窗，
怎麼見到
耀眼的陽光？

● : If we don't open the window,
how can we see the brilliant sunshine?

歡西想

The Venerable Master Hua said:

If you don't
open the gate to your mind,
even if the light of Buddha is there,
it can't shine in.

打開心，
讓佛光普照。

: So let's open our mind and let the light of Buddha shine everywhere.

Cathie's Reflections

這個世界上就是這樣，
再壞的人也有人讚歎你；
再好的人，也有人譭謗你。

這一切，
不值得你
哭泣。

● : All this is not worth crying over.

歡西想

The Venerable Master Hua said:

Such is the world:

even the worst people
are praised by some,
and even the best people
are slandered by some.

我深信，
還有許多好人存在，
還有許多好事會發生。

 : I truly believe that there are still a lot of good people around,
and a lot of good things still will happen.

Cathie's Reflections

宣公上人說

無論什麼事情，
稍微差一點，
那裏邊就有問題了，
差之絲毫，就謬之千里。

73

: Oh, no! My line was only a little bit crooked.
How come it ended up leaning totally to one side?

The Venerable Master Hua said:

Whatever the affair,
the slightest misjudgment
will embed a problem therein—and then,
"off by a hair at the beginning,
you will miss it by a thousand miles in the end."

所以啊！
就算是一點點占，
可都不能馬虎喲！

● : So we shouldn't be careless even over minor things!

Cathie's Reflections

你若 認識一切萬物
都在那兒 演說妙法，
就會一天比一天明白。

我觀察這群
勤奮工作的小螞蟻,
是不是有什麼
教導著我呢?

: As I observe this group of hard working ants,
I wonder whether there is a lesson for me to learn?

勤而想

The Venerable Master Hua said:

If you recognize
the myriad phenomena
as constantly speaking the Dharma,
then day by day
your understanding will grow.

僅管只有小小的力量，
卻仍然辛勤努力。

: Although they have only a little strength,
these ants still make an effort to work very hard.

Cathie's Reflections

你想要消災，

第一要不生煩惱，

第二要不發脾氣，

第三要不欺壓旁人。

你就顧著生氣埋怨，
前面發生了什麼事情，

你都看不見。

: If you're always angry and complaining,
　you won't be able to see what's happening in front of you.

凱西想

The Venerable Master Hua said:

If you wish disasters to be dispelled,
you must first refrain from getting afflicted;
second, you must not get angry;
and third, you must not oppress others.

靜下來吧！
把心靜下來。
不要煩惱，不要發脾氣。

● : Quiet down, and calm your mind!
   Don't worry, and don't lose your temper.

Cathie's Reflections

改過自新是個最要緊的道理，
因為你若不懂得改過自新，
那個錯總是存在的，

犯一個錯，
就像給自己
吹熄了一盞燈。

: When we make a mistake,
it is like blowing out one of our lamps.

歡西想

The Venerable Master Hua said:

To correct your mistakes and make
a fresh start is the most important
principle for cultivation,
because if you don't understand
enough to mend your ways and reform,
the mistakes will always be there.

87

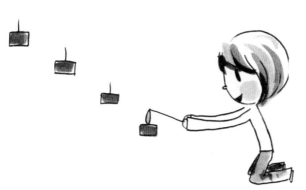

改一個過，
就像是點了盞燈。

: When we correct one mistake, it is like lighting one lamp.

Cathie's Reflections

宣公上人說

「過能改，歸於無」
不論你有什麼過錯，
你若能改這個過錯，
那前途還有光明；
如果不能改這個過錯，
那你的前途是黑暗的。

當過全改了，
燈全點亮了，
前途也就光明了。

● ： When we correct all of our mistakes,
　　 then we light all of the lamps, and our future will be bright.

凱西想

The Venerable Master Hua said:

There is a saying,
"If you correct your mistake,
then it disappears."
Therefore, no matter what kind
of faults you have,
as long as you can correct these faults,
your future is still bright.
However, if you fail to change these faults,
then your future will be dark.

尋著希望之光，
我踏上光明前程。

● ：Searching for this light of hope, I am stepping into a bright future.

Cathie's Reflections

佛 教 總 會 —— 簡稱「法總」

· 為了將佛教的真實義理，
  傳播到世界各地，
  因此，
  宣公上人在美國
  創辦了這個佛教團體。

· 我們的責任是翻譯經典、
  弘揚正法、提倡道德教育、
  利樂一切眾生。

· 我們的宗旨是不爭、不貪、不求、不自私、不自利、不妄語。

· 我們的道場除了西方佛教史上第一座大道場「萬佛聖城」外，
  還有將近三十座的分支道場，遍佈美、亞洲。

· 我們的僧眾可都要遵佛制：
  日中一食、時時披著袈裟、持戒念佛、研習經教、參禪打坐，
  大家和合地住在道場，將自己的身心性命獻給佛教。

· 我們還有國際譯經學院、法界宗教研究院、僧伽居士訓練班、
  法界佛教大學、培德中學、育良小學等譯經及教育機構。

· 我們的道場、機構，門戶開放，
  所以，凡是願意致力於仁義道德、明心見性的人士，
  都歡迎前來共同研習！

DRBA

An Introduction to the Dharma Realm Buddhist Association

- In order to disseminate the true principles of Buddhism
  to all areas of the world, the Venerable Master Hua founded
  this Buddhist organization in America.

- Our missions are to translate the Buddhist scriptures,
  to propagate the orthodox Dharma,
  to promote ethics-based education,
  and to benefit all sentient beings.

- Our guiding principles are: no contention, no greed, no seeking, no selfishness, no self-seeking, and no lying.
- In addition to the City of Ten Thousand Buddhas, which is the first large monastery in the history of Buddhism in the West, we have nearly thirty branch monasteries located throughout the United States, Canada and Asia.
- Our Sangha members honor the rules and practices established by the Buddha: eating only one meal a day, always wearing the precept sash, observing the precepts and being mindful of the Buddha, studying the Buddha's teachings, practicing meditation, living together in harmony, and dedicating their lives to Buddhism.
- Our translation and educational institutions include the International Institute for the Translation of Buddhist Texts, the Institute for World Religions, the Sangha and Laity Training Programs, Dharma Realm Buddhist University, Developing Virtue Secondary School, and Instilling Goodness Elementary School.
- All of our monasteries and institutions have an open-door policy. We welcome anyone who wishes to devote themselves to humaneness, justice, ethics, and the discovery of their true mind to come and explore these issues with us!

宣化上人 簡傳

來自白雪皚皚的長白山區。

十九歲出家修道，發願普渡一切眾生。

一九六二年將正確真實的佛法，

由東方帶到西方——美國。

創美國佛教史始有僧相之記錄——

一九六八年五位美國人在上人座下出家，

是在西方建立三寶的第一人。

建立美國第一座佛教大道場——萬佛聖城，

分支道場遍佈美加地區，乃至亞洲。

一九九五年圓寂

「我從虛空來，回到虛空去。」

終其一生儘量幫助世界走向安樂光明的途徑，

大慈悲普渡，流血汗，不休息！

A Brief Introduction to the Venerable Master Hsuan Hua

He came from the snow-laden vicinity of the Eternally
White Mountains in northeastern China.
At the age of nineteen, he became a Buddhist monk
and vowed to save all living beings.
In 1962, he brought the Proper Buddhadharma from East to West.
In 1968, five Americans took monastic vows under his guidance;
thus, he established the Sangha and the Triple Jewel on American soil.
He founded the City of Ten Thousand Buddhas,
the first large American Buddhist monastic community,
with affiliated branch monasteries in
the United States, Canada, and Asia.
In 1995, before he passed into stillness, he said,
"I came from empty space, and to empty space I will return."
Throughout his life, he promoted peace and light in the world,
compassionately and tirelessly rescuing living beings.

上人給我希望之光

也許稱不上藝術家，
但我絕對有藝術家的壞脾氣。
心不定，浮動。凡事盡往死胡同裡鑽。
再小的事也要放大了去看，
好像和自己過不去似的。
上人的「金鋼棒喝」，把我的藝術家脾氣打跑了。
上人的開示妙語如珠，越讀越明白。
淺的深的，上人說的，
開始像小豆苗般在心田裡發芽。
我藿見察周遭小事物，試著和上人說過的做一個呼應。
原來一切萬物，真的都在教導著我們啊！

The Venerable Master Gives Me a Light of Hope

By Cathie Chen

Maybe I should not claim to be an artist,
but I definitely have a diva's bad temper.
Also, my mind wanders; and in everything that I do,
I end up meandering into dead-end alleys.
I make a big deal out of even the smallest thing.
It is as if I am incapable of letting myself be a little more at ease.
Fortunately, the warning of the Venerable Master's "Vajra Staff"
chased away my bad temper.
The Venerable Master's teachings contain countless,
wondrous statements; the more I read,
the more I understand. Both the easier and the more difficult concepts
in the Venerable Master's teachings are like little seedlings beginning
to sprout in my mind.
I observe little things around me
and try to see how they correspond to the Venerable Master's teachings.
I realize that there is a lesson for us to learn in everything
that we encounter!

我知錯了！

I know my mistakes now!

接著我也讀了些上人對經典的淺釋；
也終於透過錄音帶，聽見上人的聲音。
第一次聽見上人的聲音，忍不住淚流滿面，
我這個壞孩子，也有機會受到上人的教化，
真是非常大的福報啊！
如果說連我這種超級難教化的「藝術家」，
都有一絲改過向善的希望，
那麼，人人皆成佛，便只是時間的問題啦！
那麼，我們便從這本小書做為開端，
領受上人的教育吧！

I then read some of the Venerable Master's commentaries
on the Sutras (Buddhist scriptures),
and finally heard his voice on cassette tapes.
The first time I heard the Venerable Master's voice,
tears ran down my face.
Even a bad child like me has the opportunity to receive
the Venerable Master's teachings.
I really have a lot of blessings!
If a super-hard-to-teach "artist" like me has a hope
of correcting mistakes and changing for the better,
then everyone can attain Buddhahood;
it is just a matter of time! Let's use this little book as a start
to receive the Venerable Master's teachings!

Cathie's Reflections

法界佛教總會 · 萬佛聖城
Dharma Realm Buddhist Association &
The City of Ten Thousand Buddhas
4951 Bodhi Way, Ukiah, CA 95482 U.S.A.
Tel: (707) 462-0939   Fax: (707) 462-0949

國際譯經學院
The International Translation Institute
1777 Murchison Drive
Burlingame, CA 94010-4504 U.S.A.
Tel: (650) 692-5912   Fax: (650) 692-5056

法界宗教研究院（柏克萊寺）
Institute for World Religions
(at Berkeley Buddhist Monastery)
2304 McKinley Avenue, Berkeley, CA 94703 U.S.A
Tel: (510) 848-3440   Fax: (510) 548-4551

金山聖寺 **Gold Mountain Monastery**
800 Sacramento Street
San Francisco, CA 94108 U.S.A.
Tel: (415) 421-6117   Fax: (415) 788-6001

金聖寺 **Gold Sage Monastery**
11455 Clayton Road, San Jose, CA 95127 U.S.A.
Tel: (408) 923-7243   Fax: (408) 923-1064

法界聖城 **City of the Dharma Realm**
1029 West Capitol Avenue
West Sacramento, CA 95691 U.S.A.
Tel: (916) 374-8268   Fax: (916) 374-8234

金輪聖寺 **Gold Wheel Monastery**
235 North Avenue 58
Los Angeles, CA 90042-4207 U.S.A.
Tel: (323) 258-6668   Fax: (323) 258-3619

長堤聖寺 **Long Beach Monastery**
3361 East Ocean Boulevard
Long Beach, CA 90803 U.S.A.
Tel/Fax: (562) 438-8902

福祿壽聖寺
Blessings, Prosperity, and Longevity Monastery
4140 Long Beach Boulevard
Long Beach, CA 90807 U.S.A.
Tel/Fax: (562) 595-4966

金峰聖寺 **Gold Summit Monastery**
233 First Avenue West
Seattle, WA 98119 U.S.A.
Tel: (206) 284-6690   Fax: (206) 284-6918

金佛聖寺 **Gold Buddha Monastery**
248 E. 11th Avenue, Vancouver
B.C. V5T 2C3 Canada
Tel: (604) 709-0248   Fax: (604) 684-3754

華嚴聖寺 **Avatamsaka Monastery**
1009 Fourth Avenue S.W.,
Calgary, AB T2P 0K8 Canada
Tel/Fax: (403) 234-0644

華嚴精舍 Avatamsaka Vihara ·
9601 Seven Locks Road Bethesda, MD 20817-9997 U.S.A.
Tel: (301) 469-8300

美國法界佛教總會駐華辦事處（法界佛教印經會）Dharma Realm Buddhist Books Distribution Society
臺灣省臺北市忠孝東路六段 85 號 11 樓
11th Floor, 85 Chung-Hsiao E. Road, Sec. 6, Taipei, R.O.C.
Tel: (02) 2786-3022, 2786-2474   Fax: (02) 2786-2674

法界聖寺 Dharma Realm Sagely Monastery
臺灣省高雄縣六龜鄉興龍村東溪山莊 20 號
20, Tung-hsi Shan-chuang, Hsing-lung Village, Liu-Kuei, Kaohsiung County, Taiwan, R.O.C.
Tel: (07) 689-3713   Fax: (07) 689-3870

彌陀聖寺 Amitabha Monastery
臺灣省花蓮縣壽豐鄉池南村四健會 7 號
7, Su-chien-hui, Chih-nan Village, Shou-Feng,
Hualien County, Taiwan, R.O.C.
Tel: (03) 865-1956   Fax: (03) 865-3426

般若觀音聖寺（原紫雲洞）
Prajna Guan Yin Sagely Monastery
(formerly Tze Yun Tung Temple)
Batu 5 1/2, Jalan Sungai Besi, Salak Selatan,
57100 Kuala Lumpur, Malaysia
Tel: (03)7982-6560   Fax: (03) 7980-1272

法界觀音聖寺（登彼岸）
Kun Yam Thong Temple (Deng Bi An)
161, Jalan Ampang, 50450 Kuala Lumpur, Malaysia
Tel: (03) 2164-8055   Fax: (03) 2163-7118

宣化上人衣裏明珠系列

Pearls of Wisdom by the Venerable Master Hua: A Series

有顆無價的寶珠，生生世世未曾與你捨離。
你，不該對它陌生；但是，你，認識它嗎？
無論如何，不能再不認識它！
且讓宣公上人帶著你，
找回這顆猶如藏在衣裏深處，被遺忘的明珠。

There is a priceless,

precious jewel that is always with you, life after life.

You should not be a stranger to it. However, do you recognize it?

More than anything else, it is important that you recognize it now!

Let the Venerable Master Hua lead you to rediscover

this neglected precious jewel that you have always carried with you,

even without knowing it.

朝露 Dew Drops

出塵 Transcending the World

珍惜 Cherish Your Body

清心 Pure Mind (in Chinese only)

萬佛城・萬佛成
Ten Thousand Buddhas City
accomplishes Ten Thousand Buddhas

國家圖書館出版品預行編目資料

希望之光 = The light of hope ／宣化上人作
；凱西‧陳插畫，——初版，——臺北市；法總
中文部, 2006〔民 95〕印刷
面： 公分.——（衣裏明珠：6）
中英對照
ISBN 986-7328-25-6（平裝）
1.佛教—語錄
225.4   95000572

希望之光
the Light of Hope

作　者　宣化上人
插　畫　凱西.陳

發行人　法界佛教總會　佛經翻譯委員會　法界佛教大學
　　　　Dharma Realm Buddhist Association &
　　　　The City of Ten Thousand Buddhas （萬佛聖城）
地　址　4951 Bodhi Way, Ukiah, CA 95482 U.S.A.
　　　　Tel: (707) 462-0939　Fax: (707) 462-0949

出　版　法界佛教總會中文出版部
地　址　台灣省台北市忠孝東路六段 85 號 11 樓
　　　　Tel: (02) 2786-3022　Fax: (02) 2786-2674

倡　印　法界佛教印經會
　　　　地址／電話：同上

　　　　法界文教基金會
　　　　台灣省高雄縣六龜鄉興龍村東溪山莊 20 號

出版日　2006 年 1 月 28 日／華嚴菩薩聖誕　初版五刷
ISBN 986-7328-25-6
www.drba.org／www.drbachinese.org